|| Dedicated to all wisdom seekers around the World ||

ꕥ

SECRETS TO CREATE A LIFE OF ABUNDANCE

STRATEGIES FOR ACHIEVING FINANCIAL FREEDOM

DR. JAGADEESH PILLAI

Made with ❤ on the Notion Press Platform
www.notionpress.com

Contents

Contents

PRYAER

"Om Bhadram Karnebhih Shrunuyaama DevaahBhadram Pashyemaakshabhiryajatraah SthirairangaistushtuvaamsastanoobhihVyashema Devahitam YadaayuhSwasti Na Indro VridhashravaahSwasti Nah Pooshaa VishwavedaahSwasti Nastaarkshyo ArishtanemihSwasti No Brihaspatir DadhaatuOm Shantih, Shantih, Shantih"

The literal meaning of this mantra is: OM. O Gods! Let us hear auspicious words from our ears. O reverent Gods! Let us behold propitious visions from our eyes, let our organs and body be stable, healthy, and strong. Let us do that which is pleasing to the gods in the life span allotted to us. May Indra, inscribed in the scriptures, bring us fortune! May Pushan, the knower of the world, grant us prosperity! May Trakshya, who vanquishes enemies, bestow us with blessings! May Brihaspati bring us success!
OM Peace, Peace, Peace.

About The Author

Dr. Jagadeesh Pillai is a renowned Guinness World Record holder, writer, and researcher hailing from Varanasi, also known as the abode of Lord Shiva. With a Ph.D. in Vedic Science and a range of creative ideas and achievements, he is a true polymath. He is the author of more than 100 books including Research Publications. Although his roots can be traced back to Kerala, the people of Varanasi hold him in high regard and affectionately consider him one of their own.

In 1998, Dr. Pillai was offered a job at Banaras Hindu University, but he left the position after only two months to pursue greater goals in life. He believed that in order to study Indian scriptures and engage in other creative endeavours, he needed to retire from the daily grind of working solely for money at a young age.

He started an export business from scratch, using the knowledge he had gained from a previous job in the industry. His intelligence and unique approach to business led to great success in a short period of time, earning him more in just a decade and a half than he would have in a lifetime working in a government job. Upon the passing of Dr. APJ Abdul Kalam, Dr. Pillai decided to leave the business and dedicate himself to reading, studying, researching, and experimenting.

During his tenure in the export business, Dr. Pillai traveled to over 16 countries, gaining valuable insight and experiencing the world and life in detail.

Dr. Pillai has achieved four Guinness World Records in the following subjects:

"Script to Screen" - In this record, Dr. Pillai produced and directed an animation film within the shortest time possible, breaking the previous record set by Canadians. He has also received numerous national and international awards and recognitions for this achievement.

Longest Line of Postcards - For this record, Dr. Pillai created a line of 16,300 postcards on the occasion of the 163rd anniversary of Indian Postal Day. The event also included a questionnaire about the Indian flag.

Largest Poster Awareness Campaign - Dr. Pillai designed an awareness campaign on the subject of "Beti Bachao - Beti Padhao" (Save the Girl Child - Educate the Girl Child) to achieve this record.

Largest Envelope - In tribute to the Indian Prime Minister's "Make in India" initiative, Dr. Pillai created a 4000 square meter envelope using waste paper to achieve this record.

Attempted - **70000 Candles on a 210 kg Cake** - To celebrate the 70th Indian Independence Day, Dr. Pillai attempted to light 70,000 candles on a 210 kg cake, which was recorded in World Records India.

Attempted - **Documentary on Dhamek Stupa of Sarnath in 17 Languages** - Dr. Pillai attempted to create a documentary on the Dhamek Stupa of Sarnath, dubbing it in 17 different languages. The result of this attempt is currently awaiting confirmation from the Guinness World Records.

Dr. Pillai is skilled in teaching the Bhagavad Gita, a Hindu scripture, and is popular among young people. He has helped many young people improve their lives through his motivational teachings.

In addition to teaching, he has composed and sung numerous Sanskrit Bhajans and patriotic songs.

He has also written and directed several short films and documentaries for awareness campaigns, and has volunteered with the police in both UP and Kerala to spread awareness about various issues through videos and photography.

Incredibly, he has produced and directed over 100 documentaries about the city of Varanasi, all on his own.

He has also helped and guided more than 25 boys and girls to achieve world records through creative and innovative methods. He is a multifaceted person who uses his intellect and the blessings given to him by God to excel in various areas. He is both a teacher and a student, always learning and teaching, and is able to master any subject he comes across.

He is a selfless social activist and motivational speaker who has overcome struggles and failures to become a successful and enthusiastic individual with a rich life experience.

In addition to his work with the Bhagavad Gita, he is also an efficient Tarot card reader, Astro-Vastu consultant, and a talented singer and composer. He has sung the entire Ram Charita Manas and Bhagavad Gita in his own compositions, and has sung the phrase "Lokah Samastha Sukhino Bhavantu" in 50 different languages. He is currently working on a detailed and scientific study of Vedas, Upanishads, Puranas, and the Bhagavad Gita. He has also composed and sung the Hanuman Chalisa and Gayatri Mantra in 108 and 1008 different compositions, respectively.

Awards - Four Times Guinness World Records, Winner of Mahatma Gandhi Vishwa Shanti Puraskar, Mahatma Gandhi Global Peace Ambassador, Kashi Ratna Award, Dr. APJ Abdul Kalam Motivational Person of the Year 2017, Mother Teresa Award, Indira Gandhi Priyadarshini Award, Bharat Vikas Ratna Award, Udyog Ratna Award, Vigyan Prasar Award, Poorvanchal Ratn Samman.

Preface

Welcome to "Secrets to Create a Life of Abundance: Strategies for Achieving Financial Freedom." This book was written with the goal of providing you with the knowledge and tools necessary to achieve financial stability and build a life of abundance.

In today's fast-paced world, it's easy to get caught up in the daily grind and put your financial goals on the backburner. However, taking control of your finances is an essential step towards creating the life you want. Whether you're looking to retire comfortably, save for a major life event, or simply build a solid financial foundation, this book will provide you with the guidance and strategies you need to get there.

Throughout the chapters, you will learn about different aspects of personal finance, including developing a savings strategy, creating a retirement plan, optimizing your tax strategy, establishing a financial legacy, setting your financial priorities, and more. You'll also discover the importance of managing your cash flow and understanding insurance basics, as well as how to plan for major life events, such as marriage, having children, and buying a home.

By following the strategies outlined in this book, you'll gain the confidence and knowledge necessary to make informed financial decisions and take control of your financial future. Whether you're just starting out or have been working on your finances for a while, "Secrets to Create a Life of Abundance" will provide you with the tools and insights you need to achieve financial freedom and build a life of abundance.

So let's get started! In the following chapters, you'll discover the secrets to creating a life of abundance and taking control of your financial future. Whether you're looking to retire comfortably, save for a major life event, or simply build a solid financial foundation, this book will provide you with the guidance and strategies you need to get there.

I

Understanding Your Financial Goals

In order to create a life of abundance and achieve financial freedom, it's crucial to have a clear understanding of your financial goals. Your financial goals are the end-result you hope to achieve with your money. These goals can range from short-term aims, such as paying off debt or saving for a down payment on a house, to long-term aspirations, such as building wealth or planning for retirement.

It's important to take the time to reflect on your values, aspirations, and priorities to determine what your financial goals should be. This process can be done by asking yourself a series of questions, such as:

What are your long-term aspirations in life?

What financial resources will you need to achieve these aspirations?

How much money will you need to live comfortably in the future?

What are your immediate financial needs, such as paying off debt, building an emergency fund, or buying a home?

What kind of legacy would you like to leave for future generations?

Once you have a clear understanding of your financial goals, it's important to prioritize them. This means focusing on the most important goals first and putting less emphasis on the less important ones. For example, if you have high-interest debt, it may be wise to focus on paying it off before saving for retirement or investing in the stock market.

It's also important to have specific, measurable, and achievable financial goals. For example, instead of simply stating that you want to save money, set a goal to save a specific amount of money each month, such as $500. This will give you a tangible target to work towards, making it easier to track your progress and stay motivated.

In addition to setting financial goals, it's important to have a plan for achieving them. This can include developing a budget, creating an investment plan, and seeking professional advice if necessary. With the right mindset, a well-defined plan, and consistent effort, you can achieve your financial goals and create a life of abundance.

In conclusion, understanding your financial goals is a critical step in achieving financial freedom. By reflecting on your values, aspirations, and priorities, you can determine what your goals should be, prioritize them, and develop a plan for achieving them. With a clear understanding of your financial goals, you can make informed decisions about your money and take control of your financial future.

"The key to creating a life of abundance is to develop strategies for achieving financial freedom."

ജ

II

Building Your Emergency Fund

An emergency fund is an essential component of achieving financial freedom and creating a life of abundance. An emergency fund is a savings account specifically designated for unexpected expenses, such as job loss, medical bills, or home repairs. Without an emergency fund, you may be forced to rely on credit cards or high-interest loans to pay for unexpected expenses, which can quickly spiral out of control and negatively impact your financial situation.

The first step in building an emergency fund is to determine how much you need to save. A common guideline is to have three to six months' worth of living expenses saved. To determine your monthly living expenses, start by creating a budget that includes all of your fixed expenses, such as rent or mortgage payments, utilities, transportation, and insurance. Additionally, factor in your variable expenses, such as food, entertainment, and clothing. Once you have a clear understanding of your monthly living expenses, you can calculate the total amount you would need to live for three to six months.

The next step is to determine how much you can afford to save each month. This may involve making changes to your budget, such as cutting back on discretionary spending or increasing your income. The key is to find a balance between saving for your emergency fund and still enjoying life.

Once you have determined the amount you need to save and how much you can afford to save each month, it's time to start building your emergency fund. This can be done by opening a savings account specifically designated for your emergency fund and automating your monthly contributions. By automating your contributions, you won't have to think about transferring money into your emergency fund each month, and you'll be less likely to spend the money on something else.

It's also important to consider the type of account you use for your emergency fund. A savings account is typically the best option, as it offers a low-risk way to earn interest on your savings while still providing easy access to your funds in case of an emergency.

In conclusion, building an emergency fund is an important step in achieving financial freedom and creating a life of abundance. By determining how much you need to save, finding a balance between saving and spending, and automating your contributions, you can ensure that you are prepared for unexpected expenses and have the financial stability to pursue your financial goals.

"Focus on the long-term and create a plan for financial success."

ཚ

III

Leveraging Debt for Financial Freedom

Debt is often seen as a burden that hinders financial freedom and creates stress and anxiety. While it's true that high-interest debt, such as credit card debt, can be harmful to your financial health, there are also types of debt that can help you achieve financial freedom. This is known as leveraging debt.

Leveraging debt is the strategic use of debt to increase your net worth and achieve your financial goals. This can include taking out a mortgage to purchase real estate, using a loan to start a business, or borrowing against your home equity to invest in the stock market.

The key to leveraging debt successfully is to ensure that the returns on your investment are greater than the interest you are paying on the debt. For example, if you take out a loan to start a business and the profits from the business are greater than the interest you are paying on the loan, then you are using debt to your advantage.

One of the most common forms of leveraging debt is using a mortgage to purchase real estate. By taking out a mortgage, you can purchase a property for a fraction of the cost, with the rest of the cost being financed through the loan. As the value of the property increases, your net worth also increases, providing you with the opportunity to build wealth over time.

It's also important to consider the terms of the loan when leveraging debt. For example, if you take out a loan with a high interest rate and long repayment period, it will take longer to achieve financial freedom and may actually harm your financial situation. On the other hand, if you take out a loan with a low interest rate and short repayment period, you can quickly pay off the debt and achieve financial freedom faster.

In conclusion, leveraging debt can be a powerful tool for achieving financial freedom and creating a life of abundance. However, it's important to use debt strategically and ensure that the returns on your investment are greater than the interest you are paying on the debt. By considering the terms of the loan and the potential returns, you can leverage debt to your advantage and achieve your financial goals faster.

"Start small and build your way up to financial freedom."

ꟸ

IV

Creating Passive Income Streams

Passive income is a type of income that requires minimal effort to maintain and provides a consistent stream of income over time. This type of income is a key component of achieving financial freedom and creating a life of abundance, as it allows you to earn money even when you are not actively working.

There are many different types of passive income streams, including rental income from real estate, dividends from stocks and mutual funds, and interest from savings accounts and bonds. Additionally, there are many other creative ways to generate passive income, such as creating and selling digital products, investing in peer-to-peer lending, and licensing your intellectual property.

One of the most important steps in creating passive income streams is to diversify your income sources. By having multiple streams of income, you can reduce the risk of relying on a single source of income, and ensure that you have a consistent and steady stream of income over time.

Another key factor in creating passive income streams is to have a long-term perspective. Creating passive income streams takes time, effort, and patience. It's important to understand that there may be some upfront investment, but over time the income from your passive income streams will grow, providing you with the financial stability to achieve your financial goals.

It's also important to consider your skills and interests when creating passive income streams. By choosing an income stream that aligns with your skills and interests, you will be more likely to be successful and enjoy the process of creating and maintaining the income stream.

In conclusion, creating passive income streams is a critical component of achieving financial freedom and creating a life of abundance. By diversifying your income sources, having a long-term perspective, and choosing an income stream that aligns with your skills and interests, you can ensure a consistent and steady stream of income over time, allowing you to achieve your financial goals and live a life of abundance.

"Invest in yourself and your future to create a life of abundance."

ꕤ

V

Analyzing Investment Opportunities

Investing is one of the most effective ways to grow your wealth and achieve financial freedom. However, with so many investment options available, it can be difficult to know where to start. In this chapter, we will provide you with a comprehensive guide to analyzing investment opportunities and making informed decisions that will help you reach your financial goals.

Step 1:Define Your Investment Goals

The first step in analyzing investment opportunities is to clearly define your investment goals. What are you hoping to achieve with your investment? Are you looking to grow your wealth over the long term or generate a steady income stream? Are you comfortable taking on higher levels of risk or would you prefer lower-risk, lower-return investments? Answering these questions will help you narrow down your investment options and determine which opportunities are best suited to your needs.

Step 2:Research the Investment Opportunity

Once you have a clear understanding of your investment goals, it's time to start researching the investment opportunity itself. This can involve looking at financial reports, reading news articles, and speaking to people who have experience with the investment. You should also consider factors such as the company's management team, its competition, and the industry it operates in.

Step 3: Evaluate the Financial Health of the Company

One of the most important aspects of analyzing investment opportunities is evaluating the financial health of the company. This involves looking at financial metrics such as revenue growth, profitability, and cash flow. You should also look at the company's debt levels and how it is financing its operations. If the company has a strong balance sheet, is profitable, and has a solid track record of growth, it may be a good investment opportunity.

Step 4: Consider the Market and Economic Conditions

In addition to the financial health of the company, it's important to consider the market and economic conditions that may impact the investment. This can include factors such as interest rates, inflation, and government policies. If the market is in a downturn or the economy is facing challenges, this may not be the best time to invest in a particular opportunity.

Step 5: Assess the Potential Risks and Rewards

Finally, it's important to assess the potential risks and rewards of the investment opportunity. This includes considering the likelihood of the investment losing value, as well as the potential for growth and returns. Understanding the risks and rewards of an investment will help you make informed decisions and determine whether it is the right opportunity for you.

Conclusion By following these steps and conducting thorough research and analysis, you can make informed investment decisions that will help you achieve your financial goals. Investing can be a complex process, but by taking the time to understand the opportunities available and evaluating their potential risks and rewards, you can maximize your chances of success and create a life of abundance and financial freedom.

"Take calculated risks to reach your financial goals."

ℵ

VI

Growing Your Net Worth

Net worth is a key metric for measuring one's financial well-being. It is calculated by subtracting liabilities from assets. As you grow your net worth, you increase your financial stability and reduce your dependence on debt. The more your net worth grows, the closer you are to financial freedom.

In this chapter, we'll explore some strategies for growing your net worth, so that you can create a life of abundance and achieve financial freedom.

Start by tracking your net worth.

To grow your net worth, you first need to know what it is. Create a balance sheet that lists all your assets (including cash, investments, real estate, and personal property) and all your liabilities (including credit card debt, student loans, and mortgages). Track your net worth regularly so you can monitor your progress.

Increase your income.

The first step in growing your net worth is to increase your income. You can do this by finding a better-paying job, starting a side hustle, or investing in real estate or other income-generating assets. Consider taking courses or getting certifications to increase your earning potential.

Reduce your expenses.

Cutting expenses is an effective way to increase your savings and grow your net worth. Look for areas where you can reduce your spending, such as eating out, shopping, and entertainment. Consider creating a budget and sticking to it. You can also reduce expenses by consolidating debt and negotiating bills.

Invest in the stock market.

Investing in the stock market is one of the best ways to grow your net worth. It is important to have a well-diversified portfolio and to understand the risks involved. Consider consulting a financial advisor if you are unsure about which stocks to invest in.

Invest in real estate.

Real estate can also be a great way to grow your net worth. You can invest in rental property, flip houses, or invest in real estate investment trusts (REITs). Again, it is important to understand the risks involved and to consult a financial advisor if necessary.

Start a business.

Starting a business can be a great way to increase your income and grow your net worth. Look for opportunities in areas you are passionate about and have experience in. Consider seeking advice from successful entrepreneurs and seeking out resources such as business incubators and accelerators.

Minimize debt.

Reducing debt is key to growing your net worth. The less debt you have, the more money you have to invest and save. Consider paying off high-interest debt first and then working on paying off the rest.

In conclusion, growing your net worth is a gradual process that takes time, effort, and discipline. By increasing your income, reducing expenses, investing in the stock market and real estate, starting a business, and minimizing debt, you can create a life of abundance and achieve financial freedom. Remember to track your net worth regularly and make changes as necessary to continue on the path to financial success.

"Be mindful of your spending habits and create a budget that works for you."

ꕤ

VII

Developing A Saving Strategy

Saving is a critical component of achieving financial freedom and building wealth. However, for many people, saving can be challenging. It is easy to get caught up in day-to-day expenses and to prioritize short-term wants over long-term needs. In this chapter, we will discuss strategies for developing a saving plan that will help you build wealth and achieve financial freedom.

Set realistic goals.

The first step in developing a saving strategy is to set goals. What do you want to save for? A down payment on a home? A child's education? Retirement? The more specific and meaningful your goals are, the easier it will be to stay motivated. Make sure your goals are realistic and achievable.

Create a budget.

A budget is a crucial tool for saving. A budget helps you understand where your money is going and where you can cut expenses. It also helps you determine how much you can realistically save each month. Consider using a budgeting app or spreadsheet to track your expenses and income.

Automate your savings.

One of the easiest ways to save is to automate the process. Set up a direct deposit from your paycheck into a savings account. This way, you never see the money and are less likely to spend it. You can also set up automatic transfers from your checking account to your savings account.

Pay yourself first.

Another effective strategy is to pay yourself first. When you get your paycheck, transfer a portion of it into a savings account before paying any bills. This way, you are guaranteed to save a certain amount each month.

Minimize debt.

Debt can be a major drain on your savings. The interest you pay on credit cards and other loans can quickly add up. Minimize debt by paying off high-interest debt first and then focusing on paying off the rest. Consider negotiating with creditors for lower interest rates or seeking the advice of a financial advisor.

Live below your means.

Living below your means is key to saving. This means spending less than you earn and avoiding lifestyle inflation.

Look for ways to reduce your expenses, such as cooking at home, carpooling, and using coupons.

Invest in a 401(k) or IRA.

Investing in a retirement account, such as a 401(k) or IRA, can be a great way to save. Contributions to these accounts are tax-deductible, and the money grows tax-free. Consider contributing the maximum amount allowed by law.

Take advantage of employer matching programs.

Many employers offer matching programs for 401(k)s. This means that they will match a portion of your contributions. Take advantage of this free money by contributing enough to get the full match.

In conclusion, developing a saving strategy is a critical step in achieving financial freedom. By setting realistic goals, creating a budget, automating your savings, paying yourself first, minimizing debt, living below your means, investing in a retirement account, and taking advantage of employer matching programs, you can build wealth and achieve financial security. Remember, saving takes time and discipline, but the reward is worth it.

"Set realistic goals and take action to achieve them."

ꕤ

VIII

Creating A Retirement Plan

Retirement is a time in life when people hope to have enough financial security to enjoy their golden years without worry. Creating a retirement plan is essential for achieving that financial security and ensuring that you have enough money saved to last throughout your retirement years.

Determine your retirement goals.

The first step in creating a retirement plan is to determine what you want your retirement to look like. Do you want to travel? Start a new business? Live in a certain location? Your goals will help you determine how much money you need to save.

Assess your current financial situation.

Next, assess your current financial situation. This includes your income, expenses, debt, and assets. This information will help you determine how much money you need to save each month to reach your retirement goals.

Use retirement calculators.

Retirement calculators can be a useful tool in determining how much money you need to save each month to reach your retirement goals. There are many online calculators available for free, and financial advisors can also assist you in determining how much you need to save.

Consider your retirement age.

The age at which you retire will impact your retirement savings. If you plan to retire earlier, you will need to save more each month to ensure you have enough money saved. On the other hand, if you plan to work longer, you can save less each month.

Consider your retirement lifestyle.

Your retirement lifestyle will impact your retirement savings. If you plan to have a more expensive lifestyle, you will need to save more each month. If you plan to live a more modest lifestyle, you can save less each month.

Maximize your retirement savings.

Maximizing your retirement savings is crucial. Consider investing in a 401(k) or IRA, which can help you save for retirement and reduce your taxable income. Make sure you are contributing enough to get the full employer match, and consider increasing your contributions each year.

Diversify your investments.

Diversifying your investments can help reduce risk and increase your potential for growth. Consider investing in a mix of stocks, bonds, and real estate to create a well-diversified portfolio.

Review your plan regularly.

Your retirement plan should be reviewed regularly, at least once a year. This will help ensure that you are on track to reach your retirement goals and make any necessary changes.

In conclusion, creating a retirement plan is essential for achieving financial security in retirement. By determining your retirement goals, assessing your current financial situation, using retirement calculators, considering your retirement age and lifestyle, maximizing your retirement savings, diversifying your investments, and reviewing your plan regularly, you can ensure that you have enough money saved to last throughout your retirement years. Start planning today and enjoy a worry-free retirement tomorrow.

"Be disciplined and consistent in your approach to financial freedom."

ꙮ

IX

Optimizing Your Tax Strategy

Taxes can have a significant impact on your financial situation and overall net worth. Optimizing your tax strategy is an important step in achieving financial freedom and maximizing your wealth.

Understand the tax laws and regulations.

The first step in optimizing your tax strategy is to understand the tax laws and regulations that apply to you. This includes knowledge of your tax bracket, deductions, and credits, as well as any changes to the tax code.

Keep accurate records.

Accurate record-keeping is crucial in optimizing your tax strategy. Keep receipts, invoices, and any other documents that support your deductions and credits. This will make it easier to prepare your tax return and ensure that you are taking advantage of all the tax benefits available to you.

Take advantage of deductions and credits.

Deductions and credits can significantly reduce your tax liability. Common deductions include mortgage interest, charitable contributions, and business expenses. Common credits include the earned income tax credit, child tax credit, and education credits.

Consider adjusting your withholding.

Withholding too much from your paycheck can result in a large refund at tax time, but it also means that you are giving the government an interest-free loan with your money. Consider adjusting your withholding so that you are not overpaying taxes and have more money available throughout the year.

Make strategic investments.

Investing in tax-advantaged accounts, such as a 401(k) or IRA, can help you save for retirement while reducing your taxable income. Consider investing in a taxable investment account if you need access to your money before retirement age.

Consider hiring a tax professional.

A tax professional can provide valuable advice and help you navigate the tax laws and regulations. They can help you find deductions and credits you may have missed, and ensure that your tax return is accurate and up-to-date.

Review your tax strategy regularly.

Tax laws and regulations change frequently, and your financial situation may change as well. Regularly reviewing your tax strategy will help ensure that you are taking advantage of all the tax benefits available to you and maximizing your wealth.

In conclusion, optimizing your tax strategy is an important step in achieving financial freedom and maximizing your wealth. By understanding the tax laws and regulations, keeping accurate records, taking advantage of deductions and credits, adjusting your withholding, making strategic investments, and regularly reviewing your tax strategy, you can reduce your tax liability and keep more money in your pocket. Start optimizing your tax strategy today and take control of your financial future.

"Focus on building wealth, not just accumulating money."

ꟹ

X

Establishing a Financial Legacy

Establishing a financial legacy is an important part of achieving financial freedom and ensuring that your wealth and assets are passed down to future generations. By creating a plan for your financial legacy, you can protect your assets, provide for your loved ones, and leave a lasting impact on the world.

Create a will and estate plan.

The first step in establishing a financial legacy is to create a will and estate plan. A will outlines how you want your assets distributed after your death, while an estate plan helps ensure that your wishes are followed and your assets are protected. It is important to work with a qualified estate planning attorney to ensure that your will and estate plan are legally binding and take into account any state and federal laws.

Consider life insurance.

Life insurance can provide financial security for your loved ones after your death. Consider purchasing a life insurance policy to ensure that your family has the financial resources they need to cover expenses such as mortgage payments, college tuition, or living expenses.

Plan for retirement.

Planning for retirement is an important part of establishing a financial legacy. By saving for retirement, you can ensure that you have the financial resources you need to live comfortably in your golden years. Consider investing in tax-advantaged retirement accounts, such as a 401(k) or IRA, to maximize your savings and reduce your taxable income.

Create a trust.

A trust can provide a way to protect your assets and provide for your loved ones. Consider establishing a trust to hold your assets and ensure that they are distributed according to your wishes. A trust can also provide a way to minimize estate and gift taxes, protect your assets from creditors, and provide for charitable giving.

Plan for charitable giving.

Charitable giving can be an important part of establishing a financial legacy. Consider making a charitable donation or leaving a bequest in your will to a charitable organization that aligns with your values and causes. Charitable giving can provide a way to give back to your community, support important causes, and leave a lasting impact on the world.

Review your financial legacy plan regularly.

Your financial situation and goals may change over time, so it is important to review your financial legacy plan regularly. Consider working with a financial advisor to ensure that your plan is on track and that you are taking advantage of any opportunities to optimize your wealth and protect your assets.

In conclusion, establishing a financial legacy is an important part of achieving financial freedom and ensuring that your wealth and assets are passed down to future generations. By creating a will and estate plan, considering life insurance, planning for retirement, creating a trust, planning for charitable giving, and regularly reviewing your financial legacy plan, you can protect your assets, provide for your loved ones, and leave a lasting impact on the world. Start planning your financial legacy today and secure your financial future.

"Be proactive in your pursuit of financial freedom."

☙

XI

Setting Your Financial Priorities

Setting your financial priorities is the foundation of creating a life of abundance and achieving financial freedom. By determining what is most important to you and aligning your financial decisions with your values, you can ensure that your money is being used to support the things that matter most to you.

Assess your current financial situation.

The first step in setting your financial priorities is to assess your current financial situation. This includes evaluating your income, expenses, debts, and assets. By understanding your current financial picture, you can identify areas where you may need to make changes in order to achieve your financial goals.

Identify your values and goals.

The next step is to identify your values and goals. This includes both short-term and long-term goals, as well as the values that guide your financial decisions. Examples of financial goals may include paying off debt, saving for a down payment on a house, or building an emergency fund. Examples of values may include financial independence, giving back to your community, or supporting your family.

Create a budget.

Once you have assessed your current financial situation and identified your values and goals, the next step is to create a budget. A budget helps you allocate your income to the things that matter most to you, and can help ensure that you are spending your money in alignment with your values and goals. Consider using a budgeting tool or working with a financial advisor to create a budget that works for you.

Prioritize your expenses.

In order to make the most of your budget, it is important to prioritize your expenses. This means determining which expenses are most important to you and allocating your resources accordingly. For example, you may prioritize paying off debt, saving for an emergency fund, or investing in a retirement account.

Set realistic financial goals.

Setting realistic financial goals is an important part of setting your financial priorities. This includes setting both short-term and long-term goals that align with your values and your financial situation. Consider working with a financial advisor to set achievable financial goals and develop a plan to reach them.

Reassess and adjust your financial priorities as needed.

It is important to regularly reassess your financial priorities and adjust them as needed. Your financial situation, values, and goals may change over time, and it is important to ensure that your financial decisions reflect these changes.

In conclusion, setting your financial priorities is the foundation of creating a life of abundance and achieving financial freedom. By assessing your current financial situation, identifying your values and goals, creating a budget, prioritizing your expenses, setting realistic financial goals, and regularly reassessing and adjusting your financial priorities, you can ensure that your money is being used to support the things that matter most to you. Start setting your financial priorities today and take control of your financial future.

"Learn from your mistakes and use them to your advantage."

ℬ

XII

Implementing a Financial Plan

Implementing a financial plan is an essential step in creating a life of abundance and achieving financial freedom. By putting your financial goals and priorities into action, you can turn your financial aspirations into reality. This chapter will provide you with the information and tools you need to successfully implement your financial plan.

Develop a financial plan.

The first step in implementing a financial plan is to develop a comprehensive financial plan. This plan should take into account your current financial situation, your goals and priorities, and your long-term financial aspirations. Consider working with a financial advisor to create a financial plan that is tailored to your specific needs and circumstances.

Create an investment strategy.

A key component of implementing a financial plan is to create an investment strategy. This includes determining your risk tolerance, identifying your investment goals, and choosing the right mix of investments to help you reach your financial goals. Consider working with a financial advisor or taking a financial planning course to develop a solid investment strategy.

Automate your savings.

One of the most effective ways to ensure that you are saving enough money to reach your financial goals is to automate your savings. This means setting up automatic transfers from your checking account to your savings or investment accounts each month. This will help ensure that you are consistently saving money and working towards your financial goals.

Monitor your progress.

In order to ensure that you are making progress towards your financial goals, it is important to regularly monitor your financial situation. This includes tracking your spending, reviewing your investment portfolio, and monitoring your credit score. Consider using financial management tools or working with a financial advisor to help you monitor your progress and make necessary adjustments to your financial plan.

Adjust your plan as needed.

As you work towards your financial goals, it is important to be flexible and adjust your financial plan as needed. Your financial situation, goals, and priorities may change over time, and it is important to ensure that your financial plan reflects these changes. Consider working with a financial advisor to make necessary adjustments to your financial plan.

Stay disciplined and focused.

Finally, it is important to stay disciplined and focused as you implement your financial plan. This means sticking to your budget, avoiding impulse purchases, and avoiding unnecessary debt. By staying disciplined and focused, you can ensure that you are making progress towards your financial goals and creating a life of abundance.

In conclusion, implementing a financial plan is an essential step in creating a life of abundance and achieving financial freedom. By developing a comprehensive financial plan, creating an investment strategy, automating your savings, monitoring your progress, adjusting your plan as needed, and staying disciplined and focused, you can turn your financial aspirations into reality. Start implementing your financial plan today and take control of your financial future.

"Be patient and persistent in your journey to financial freedom."

❧

XIII

Managing Your Cash Flow

Managing your cash flow is a critical component of achieving financial freedom and creating a life of abundance. By effectively managing your income and expenses, you can ensure that you have the resources you need to reach your financial goals and maintain financial stability. This chapter will provide you with the information and tools you need to effectively manage your cash flow.

Understand your income and expenses.

The first step in managing your cash flow is to understand your income and expenses. This means creating a detailed budget that takes into account your monthly income, regular expenses, and discretionary spending. This will help you determine how much money you have available each month to put towards your financial goals.

Prioritize your expenses.

Once you have a clear understanding of your income and expenses, it is important to prioritize your expenses. This means determining which expenses are necessary and which expenses can be reduced or eliminated. Consider creating a priority list of your expenses, with the most important expenses listed first.

Implement a budget.

In order to effectively manage your cash flow, it is important to implement a budget. A budget will help you track your spending, identify areas where you can reduce your expenses, and ensure that you are putting enough money towards your financial goals. Consider using budgeting software or working with a financial advisor to create a budget that works for you.

Stay disciplined.

Staying disciplined is an essential component of effectively managing your cash flow. This means sticking to your budget, avoiding impulse purchases, and avoiding unnecessary debt. By staying disciplined, you can ensure that you are using your resources effectively and making progress towards your financial goals.

Monitor your cash flow regularly.

In order to ensure that you are effectively managing your cash flow, it is important to monitor your income and expenses regularly. This means tracking your spending, reviewing your budget, and making adjustments as needed. Consider using financial management tools or working with a financial advisor to help you monitor your cash flow.

Prepare for unexpected expenses.

Unexpected expenses can disrupt your cash flow and put a strain on your financial situation. To prepare for these types of expenses, consider setting aside a portion of your income each month into an emergency fund. This fund can be used to cover unexpected expenses and help ensure that you have the resources you need to maintain financial stability.

Invest in your financial future.

Finally, it is important to invest in your financial future. This means putting aside money each month into a retirement account, investing in stocks or other investments, or contributing to a college fund for your children. By investing in your financial future, you can ensure that you have the resources you need to reach your long-term financial goals.

In conclusion, managing your cash flow is a critical component of achieving financial freedom and creating a life of abundance. By understanding your income and expenses, prioritizing your expenses, implementing a budget, staying disciplined, monitoring your cash flow regularly, preparing for unexpected expenses, and investing in your financial future, you can effectively manage your cash flow and reach your financial goals. Start managing your cash flow today and take control of your financial future.

"Create multiple streams of income to increase your financial security."

ꟾ

XIV

Understanding Insurance Basics

Insurance is a crucial aspect of financial planning, as it provides protection against financial loss in the event of unexpected events such as death, disability, or illness. Insurance is a form of risk management, allowing individuals to transfer the risk of financial loss to an insurance company in exchange for a premium. In this chapter, we will cover the basics of insurance, including the different types of insurance, how to determine your insurance needs, and how to choose the right insurance coverage for you.

Types of Insurance There are several types of insurance, each designed to protect against different types of financial loss. The most common types of insurance include:

Life insurance: provides financial support to your loved ones in the event of your death.

Health insurance: helps cover the cost of medical expenses, including hospital stays, surgery, and prescription drugs.

Disability insurance: provides financial support in the event that you become disabled and are unable to work.

Auto insurance: protects you against financial loss in the event of an automobile accident.

Homeowners insurance: Covers damage to your home or personal property caused by events such as fire, theft, or natural disasters.

Umbrella insurance: provides additional liability coverage above and beyond your auto and homeowners insurance.

Determining your insurance needs To determine your insurance needs, it is important to consider your financial situation, your family, and your lifestyle. You should consider factors such as your age, health, income, debts, and assets when determining your insurance needs. It is also important to consider your future financial goals, such as retirement and college savings.

Choosing the right coverage When choosing insurance coverage, it is important to consider the coverage limits, deductibles, and premiums. Coverage limits determine the maximum amount that the insurance company will pay in the event of a covered loss. Deductibles determine the amount that you must pay out of pocket before the insurance company begins to pay. Premiums are the regular payments you make to the insurance company in exchange for coverage.

Working with an insurance agent Working with an insurance agent can help you determine your insurance needs, choose the right coverage, and compare insurance options. An insurance agent can also help you understand the terms and conditions of your insurance coverage, and assist you with the claims process in the event of a loss.

Reviewing and updating your insurance coverage It is important to review and update your insurance coverage regularly, as your insurance needs may change over time. This may include increasing your coverage limits, updating your beneficiaries, or changing insurance providers.

In conclusion, understanding insurance basics is an important component of achieving financial freedom and creating a life of abundance. By understanding the different types of insurance, determining your insurance needs, choosing the right coverage, working with an insurance agent, and regularly reviewing and updating your insurance coverage, you can ensure that you have the protection you need to secure your financial future. Start exploring your insurance options today and take control of your financial future.

"Be open to new ideas and opportunities to increase your wealth."

ℵ

XV

Financial Planning for Major Life Events

Life is full of unexpected twists and turns, and it is essential to be prepared for the financial impact of major life events. From buying a house to starting a family, or from retirement to death, these events can have a significant impact on your finances. In this chapter, we will explore how to financially plan for some of the most common major life events and how to ensure that you are prepared for whatever the future may bring.

Buying a House Buying a house is a major financial commitment and requires careful planning. To ensure that you are ready to take on this responsibility, you should consider factors such as your income, debts, and credit score. It is also important to calculate the costs associated with homeownership, including property taxes, maintenance, and insurance. To prepare for this major life event, it may be necessary to save for a down payment, reduce your debt, and improve your credit score.

Starting a Family Having a child is a joyous occasion, but it also brings financial responsibilities. From prenatal care to childcare, the costs associated with starting a family can be substantial. To prepare for this major life event, it is important to consider the costs of prenatal care, delivery, and childcare and to adjust your budget accordingly. It may also be necessary to start saving for your child's future, such as education or retirement.

Retirement Retirement is a time to enjoy the fruits of your labor and to live life to the fullest. However, to ensure a comfortable retirement, it is important to plan ahead and to start saving early. Factors such as your retirement goals, your current savings, and your expected expenses should all be taken into account when planning for retirement. Additionally, it may be necessary to consider factors such as inflation and market fluctuations when planning for retirement.

Death Death is a reality that we must all face, and it is important to be prepared for the financial impact that it may have on your loved ones. Life insurance is a key component of a comprehensive financial plan and can provide financial support for your loved ones in the event of your death. To ensure that you have adequate coverage, it is important to consider factors such as your income, debts, and beneficiaries when choosing life insurance.

Divorce Divorce can have a significant financial impact, as

it can result in the division of assets and debts. To prepare for this major life event, it is important to understand the financial consequences of divorce and to have a plan in place for dividing assets and debts. This may include factors such as alimony, child support, and the division of property.

Job Loss Job loss can be a major financial setback, as it can result in a loss of income and benefits. To prepare for this major life event, it is important to have an emergency fund in place, as well as a plan for finding new employment. This may include updating your resume, networking, and exploring alternative employment options.

In conclusion, major life events can have a significant financial impact, and it is essential to be prepared for these events. By considering the financial impact of these events, preparing a plan, and taking proactive steps to ensure financial stability, you can ensure that you are ready for whatever the future may bring. Start preparing for these major life events today, and create a life of abundance and financial freedom.

"Take control of your finances and create a life of abundance."

ꕤ

OTHER BOOKS OF THE AUTHOR

1. The Moments When I Met God
2. Kashiyile Theertha Pathangal
3. GURU GYAN VANI
4. Abhiprerak Gita
5. ASSI SE JAIN GHAT TAK
6. Hopelessness of Arjuna
7. The Soul and It's True Nature
8. Sense of Action (Karma)
9. Action through Wisdom
10. Action through Wisdom
11. THEORY AND PRACTICAL OF EVERY ACTION
12. LOGICAL UNDERSTANDING OF THE SUPREME
13. THE IMPERISHABLE SUPREME
14. Yatra Nishadraj se Hanuman Ghat Tak
15. Yatra Karnatak Ghat se Raja Ghat Tak
16. Yatra Pandey Ghat se Prayagraj Ghat Tak
17. Yatra Ranjendra Prasad Ghat se Dattatreya Ghat Tak
18. YaatraSindhiya Ghat se Gwaliar Ghat Tak
19. Yatra Mangala Gauri Ghat se Hanuman Gadhi Ghat Tak
20. Yatra Gaay Ghat Se Nishad Ghat Tak
21. MAA GANGA, GHATEN EVM UTSAV
22. Ganga Arti Dev Deepavali evam Any Utsav
23. Potentials of Digitalized India
24. VEDIC CONSCIOUSNESS
25. A Brief Introduction to Vedic Science
26. Kashi ke Barah Jyotirling
27. IMPACT OF MOTIVATION
28. Let's have a Milky Way Journey
29. Color Therapy in a Nutshell

30. Rigveda in a Nutshell
31. Yajurveda in a Nutshell
32. Samveda in a Nutshell
33. Atharva Veda in a Nutshell
34. Ayushman Bhava - Ayurveda
35. Srimad Bhagavad Gita and Upanishad Connection
36. Srimad Bhagavad Gita - an attempt to summarize each chapter.
37. Facts and Impact of Nakshatra
38. Astro Gems - NAVARATNA
39. Ekadashi - A Concise Overview
40. A Concise View of Hanuman Chalisa
41. Inspirational Gita
42. Nakshatraranyam
43. Summary of 18 Mahapuranas
44. Synopsis of 18 Upa Puranas
45. Rigvediya Upanishads
46. Shukla Yajurvediya Upanishads
47. Krishna Yajurvediya Upanishads
48. Samavediya Upanishads
49. Atharvavediya Upanishads
50. The Seven Great Sages
51. From Rocket Scientist to President Dr. APJ Abdul Kalam
52. The Visionary's Voice - Quotes of Dr. APJ Abdul Kalam
53. The Wisdom of Swami Vivekananda: Insights and Inspiration from a Legendary Spiritual Teacher
54. Ayurvedic Remedies from the Garden
55. Sages and Seers
56. Rising Strong – Motivational Stories of Women
57. Beyond Flames -Mystery stories of Funeral Ghat Manikarnika
58. The Origins of Tulsi: A Look at the Mythological Roots of the Plant"

59. The Holistic Cow: A Look at the Physical, Spiritual, and Cultural Importance of Cows in India
60. Arts of Healing
61. Exploring the Divine
62. Understanding Five Elements
63. The Etymology of Ram
64. Symbols of India
65. Voice of Change (About Speeches of Great Men)
66. She Speaks (About Speeches of Great Women)
67. Patriotism on Celluloid – Brief About Patriotic Films
68. The Music of Motivation: A Brief Guide to Inspirational Film Songs
69. **Unlocking the Secrets of the Dashopanishads**
70. A Cultural Mosaic
71. Ancient Traditions, Modern Minds
72. Ecos of Ancient Wisdom
73. Beneath the Surface
74. From Temples to Ashrams
75. Sages of the Subcontinent
76. The Art of Healling (Ayurveda, Yoga & Naturopathy)
77. Indian Kitchen
78. The Festivals of India
79. The Indian Epics Retold
80. The Power of Mantras
81. The Indian River Ganges
82. The Indian Architecture
83. Rites of Passage
84. The Indian Silk Road
85. The Indian Literature
86. The Indian Villages
87. The Indian Folks & Crafts
88. The Way of Buddha
89. The Ramayan of Tulsidas

90. Astrological Remedies
91. The Secret Power of Motivation
92. Secret of Developing your Inner Strength
93. The Secret Path to Motivation
94. The Art and Secret of Positive Thinking
95. The Secrets of Practicing Ethical Living
96. Indian Art and Painting
97. The Indian Herbalism
98. Bharatanatyam to Kathak
99. Exploring India's Astrological Remedies
100. The Indian Festival of Flowers
101. Indian Handicrafts
102. The Splashes of Joy – India's Colour Festival
103. The Indian Science of Astrology
104. The Indian Mythology
105. Path to Enlightenment
106. The Indian Spirituality for Children
107. Aromas of India
108. The Secrets of Healthy Relationships
109. Ancestral Ties
110. The Indian Street Food
111. Discovering America
112. The Indian Textile
113. Listening to Motivational Speeches
114. Taste of India
115. A Cultural Journey through Indian Nuptials
116. Motivational Quote for Change
117. Secret Strategies for Making Money
118. Secrets to Cultivate a Positive Mindset
119. A Tapestry of Cultures: Exploring India from Kashmir to Kanyakumari
120. Achieving Your Dreams with Resilience: Secret Strategies for Overcoming Obstacles

121. Innovative Startups - 25 Startup Ideas to Spark Your Business Creativity
122. Export Management: Strategies for Global Success
123. Exporting from India - A Step by Step Guide
124. Finance Fundamentals: Mastering Financial Management for Business Success
125. Global Growth Strategies for International Business Development
126. Marketing Mastery: Unlocking the Secrets of Modern Marketing
127. Operations Mastery: Managing the Flow of Value in Business
128. Strategic Business Management: Navigating the Modern Business Landscape
129. Human Resource Management Strategies for Building and Managing a High Performance Team
130. The Indian Landscapes and Nature: An Exploration Of India's Natural Beauty And Diversity
131. The Indian Street Performances: A Cultural Exploration of India's Street Performances
132. Affirming Your Self-Worth: Strategies for Achieving Emotional Wellbeing
133. Cultivating Self-Discipline: Secrets Methods for Achieving Your Goals
134. Embracing Change: Strategies for Adapting to Life's Challenges
135. Embracing Your Uniqueness: Secret Strategies for Living an Authentic Life
136. Finding Motivation in Despondency: Coping with Difficult Times
137. Embracing Change
138. Learning to Love Yourself
139. Managing Time for Yourself

140. Unlock the keys to Self-Motivation
141. Secret to Boost Confidence
142. Unlocking your Potential: A Path to Inner-strength & Success
143. Secrets to Develop Authentic Relationship
144. Secrets to Build a Successful Career
145. Secrets to Live with Gratitude
146. Secrets to Create a Life of Abundance
147. Secrets to Cultivate Self-Awareness
148. The Power of Helping Hands
149. Finding Your Passion
150. The Indian Mythical Creatures
151. The Indian Women Saints
152. The Wisdom of the Saints
153. "The Indian Royalty: A Cultural and Historical Exploration of India's Maharajas and their kingdom"
154. The Mystic Land: A Cultural and Spiritual Exploration of India"

CONTACT

DR. JAGADEESH PILLAI

MBA & PhD in Vedic Science

Four Times Guinness World Record Holder

Winner of Mahatma Gandhi Vishwa Shanti Puraskar and Global Peace Ambassador

Gemology, Astro & Vastu Consultant - Spiritual Counselor

Consultant for designing World Record Ideas

Efficient Tarot Card Reader

9839093003

myrichindia@gmail.com

drjagadeeshpillai@facebook

drjagadeeshpillai@instagram

jagadeeshpillai@youtube

www. JAGADEESHPILLAI.com

|| LOKAHA SAMASTHAHA SUKHINO BHAVANTU ||

ॐ

9 798889 594796

Printed by Libri Plureos GmbH in Hamburg,
Germany